Janice VanCleave's

ANIMALS

Spectacular Science Projects

JANICE VANCLEAVE'S
SPECTACULAR SCIENCE PROJECTS

Animals
Gravity
Molecules

JANICE VANCLEAVE'S
SCIENCE FOR EVERY KID SERIES

Astronomy for Every Kid
Biology for Every Kid
Chemistry for Every Kid
Earth Science for Every Kid
Math for Every Kid
Physics for Every Kid

Janice VanCleave's
ANIMALS
Spectacular Science Projects

John Wiley & Sons, Inc.
New York · Chichester · Brisbane · Toronto · Singapore

In recognition of the importance of preserving what has been written, it is a policy of John Wiley & Sons, Inc. to have books of enduring value published in the United States printed on acid-free paper, and we exert our best efforts to that end.

Design and Production by BOOKMAKERS LTD.
Illustrated by KATHLEEN McCORD

Library of Congress Cataloging-in-Publication Data

VanCleave, Janice Pratt
    [Animals]
    Janice VanCleave's animals.
            p.   cm. -- (Spectacular science projects)
    Includes index
    ISBN 0-471-55052-3
    1. Zoology projects--Juvenile literature.   I. Title.
II. Title: Animals. III. Series: VanCleave, Janice Pratt.
Janice VanCleave's spectacular science projects.
QL52.6.V36 1992
591'.078--dc20   92-25094

Printed in the United States of America
10 9 8 7 6 5 4 3

CONTENTS

Dedicated to my son,
whom I love dearly,

Russell Eugene VanCleave

Science is a search for answers. Science projects are good ways to learn more about science as you search for the answers to specific problems. This book will give you guidance and provide ideas, but you must do your part in the search by planning experiments, finding and recording information related to the problem, and organizing the data collected to find the answer to the problem. Sharing your findings by presenting your project at science fairs will be a rewarding experience if you have properly prepared the exhibit. Trying to assemble a project overnight results in frustration, and you cheat yourself out of the fun of being a science detective. Solving a scientific mystery, like solving a detective mystery, requires planning and the careful collecting of facts. The following sections provide suggestions for how to get started on this scientific quest. Start the project with curiosity and a desire to learn something new.

SELECT A TOPIC

The 20 topics in this book suggest many possible problems to solve. Each topic has one "cookbook" experiment—follow the recipe and the result is guaranteed. Approximate metric equivalents have been given after all English measurements. Try several or all of these easy experiments before choosing the topic you like best and want to know more about. Regardless of the problem you choose to solve, what you discover will make you more knowledgeable about creatures.

KEEP A JOURNAL

Purchase a bound notebook in which you will write everything relating to the project. This is your journal. It will contain your original ideas as well as ideas you get from books or from people like teachers and scientists. It will include descriptions of your experiments as well as diagrams, photographs, and written observations of all your results. Every entry should be as neat as possible and dated. Information from this journal can be used to write a report of your project, and you will want to display the journal with your completed project. A neat, orderly journal provides a complete and accurate record of your project from start to finish. It is also proof of the time you spent sleuthing out the answers to the scientific mystery you undertook to solve.

LET'S EXPLORE

This section of each chapter follows each of the 20 sample experiments and provides additional questions about the problem presented in the experiment. By making small changes to some part of the sample experiment, new results are achieved. Think about why these new results might have happened.

SHOW TIME!

You can use the pattern of the sample experiment to design your own experiments to solve the questions asked in "Let's Explore." Your own experiment should follow the sample experiment's format and include a single question about one thing, a list of necessary materials, a detailed step-by-step procedure, written results with diagrams, graphs, and charts if they seem helpful, and a conclusion answering and explaining the question. Include any information you found through research to clarify your answer. When you design your own experiments, make sure to get adult approval if supplies or procedures other than those given in this book are used. If you want to make a science fair project, study the information listed here and after each sample experiment in the book to develop your ideas into a real science fair exhibit. Use the suggestions that best apply to the project topic that you have chosen. Keep in mind that while your display represents all the work that you have done, it must tell the story of the project in such a way that it attracts and holds the interest of the viewer. So keep it simple. Do not try to cram all your information into one place. To have more space on the display and still exhibit all your work, keep some of the charts, graphs, pictures, and other materials in your journal instead of on the display board itself.

The actual size and shape of displays can be different, depending on the local science fair officials, so you will have to check the rules for your science fair. Most exhibits are allowed to be 48 inches (122 cm) wide, 30 inches (76 cm) deep, and 108 inches (274 cm) high. These are maximum measurements and your display may be smaller than this. A three-sided backboard (see drawing) is usually the best way to display your work. Wooden panels can be hinged together, but you can also use sturdy cardboard pieces taped together to form a very inexpensive but presentable exhibit.

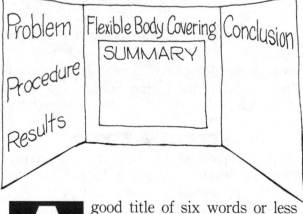

A good title of six words or less with a maximum of 50 characters should be placed at the top of the center panel. The title should capture the theme of the project but should not be the same as the problem statement. For example, if the problem under question is "Why is the skin of animals wrinkled at the joints?" a good title for the project might be "Flexible Body Covering." The title and other headings should be neat and large enough to be readable at a distance of about 3 feet (1 meter). You can glue letters on to the backboard (you can use precut letters that you buy or letters that you cut out of construction paper), or you can stencil the letters for all the titles. A short summary paragraph of about 100 words to explain the scientific principles involved is good and can be printed under the title. A person who has no knowledge of the topic should be able to easily understand the basic idea of the project just from reading the summary.

There are no set rules about the position of the information on the display. However, it all needs to be well organized, with the title and summary paragraph as the main point at the top of the center panel and the remaining material placed neatly from left to right under specific headings. Choices of headings will depend on how you wish to display the information. Separate headings for Problem, Procedure, Results, and Conclusion may be used.

The judges give points for how clearly you are able to discuss the project and explain its purpose, procedure, results, and conclusion. The display should be organized so that it explains everything, but your ability to discuss your project and answer the questions of the judges convinces them that you did the work and understand what you have done. Practice a speech in front of friends, and invite them to ask you questions. If you do not know the answer to a question, never guess or make up an answer or just say, "I do not know." Instead, you can say that you did not discover that answer during your research and then offer other information that you found of interest about the project. Be proud of the project and approach the judges with enthusiasm about your work.

CHECK IT OUT!

Read about your topic in many books and magazines. You are more likely to have a successful project if you are well informed about the topic. For the topics in this book, some tips are provided about specific places to look for information. Record in your journal all the information you find, and include for each source the author's name, the name of the book, the numbers of the pages you read, the publisher's name, where it was published, and the year of publication.

INSTANT FLIES

PROBLEM

Can worms grow from decaying bananas?

MATERIALS
masking tape
marking pen
2 1-quart (1 liter) jars
banana

PROCEDURE
Note: This experiment works best during warm weather.

1. Use the tape and marking pen to label the jars #1 and #2.

2. Peel the banana and place the fruit inside jar #2.

3. Leave the jars open and undisturbed for two weeks.

4. Observe and record your observations daily. Things to look for:

- changes in the color of the banana
- any insects, such as flies, inside the jars
- presence of maggots

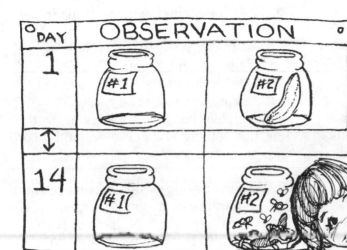

RESULTS

You can use a chart like the one shown to record your daily observations for fourteen days. It will indicate the exact day that these results were observed:

- Brown spots appeared on the banana.
- The entire banana looked dark brown and moist.
- Flies appeared and were seen inside each jar. (Record about how many flies.)
- The maggots appeared.

WHY?

Because maggots appeared in the jar with the rotting fruit and not in the empty jar, a popular theory until the eighteenth century was that living organisms such as maggots came from dead matter. The theory that living organisms come from nonliving material is called **spontaneous generation.** This theory was disproved about 100 years ago, and, through further experimentation, it was proved that gases released by the rotting fruit attract the flies. The flies lay their eggs in the fruit, and the eggs hatch into tiny, white worms called maggots. Given enough time, the maggots grow into adult flies. Thus, the maggots observed in the jar with the fruit are just one stage in the life of a fly.

LET'S EXPLORE

1. Would the maggots appear if the jar with the banana was closed? Repeat the experiment with a third jar. Label it jar #3 and place a peeled banana in it. Seal jar #3 with a lid. Observe and record the daily results.

2. Does the limited amount of air in jar #3 prevent spontaneous generation? Repeat the experiment, but this time seal jar #3 by putting a cotton handkerchief over the mouth of the jar and securing it with a rubber band. (You use a handkerchief because it allows air in the jar, but nothing else.) Observe and record the daily results.

3. Will the rotting of other fruits result in the appearance of maggots? Repeat this experiment replacing the banana with other fruit. Keep daily records of your observations for display.

SHOW TIME!

1. Use the procedure of a famous experiment designed by Francesco Redi (1626–1697) to confirm that decaying food does not produce living organisms. Place small pieces of fruit in three separate jars. Leave one jar open, seal one with a lid, and cover the third jar with a cotton handkerchief. Keep daily records of your observations for display. Find out more

the wheat grains together in a dark container.
2. Wait several days.
3. Yields many mice.

about Redi's experiment and use it in your project report.

2. Use biology texts to discover different popular spontaneous-generation beliefs, and represent them with drawings. A recipe for producing mice was created by a man named Van Helmont. It is given below. The drawing shows an example of how this can be used as part of a project display.

Note: Do not try this at home!

Van Helmont's Recipe for Mice
INGREDIENTS
1 dark container
1 cup (250 ml) wheat grains
1 dirty shirt

DIRECTIONS
1. Put the dirty shirt and

CHECK IT OUT!

Antonie van Leeuwenhoek's discovery of microorganisms made scientists question whether these tiny creatures that appeared so quickly in rotting food might arise spontaneously. Discover how an Italian priest named Lazzaro Spallanzani tried to disprove this. Why was his experiment not respected by other scientists?

BLINKERS

PROBLEM

Is blinking a reflex action (an action that does not require thinking)?

MATERIALS

helper
1 sheet of transparent
    plastic wrap
10 cotton balls

PROCEDURE

Note: Do not substitute materials. It would be unsafe to use anything other than cotton balls.

1. Have your helper hold the transparent plastic wrap in front of his or her face.

2. Stand about 1 yard (1 meter) away from your helper.

3. Without warning, throw a cotton ball directly at your helper's face. The cotton ball will be stopped by the plastic wrap.

4. Continue throwing the cotton balls, one at a time, at your helper's face.

5. Observe and record when the thrown cotton balls cause your helper to blink.

RESULTS

Your helper will be more likely to blink when the first few cotton balls are thrown. After that, he or she may be able to concentrate on keeping the eyes open and, thus, not blink after getting used to the approaching balls.

WHY?

Reflex action, such as blinking, is an automatic action that does not require thinking, and it takes concentration to try to **inhibit** (keep from happening) the

involuntary action. Some people can better control the blinking response if they are aware that the **stimuli** (anything that causes a response—the thrown cotton balls in this experiment) are coming. If a sudden unexpected object approaches, the eyelids of all creatures will blink automatically. This involuntary movement is due to

sensory cells in the eye sending a message to a central control center in the spine. From the spine, the instructions to close the eyes for protection are immediately relayed to the eye muscles resulting in the blinking action.

LET'S EXPLORE

Would the reflex response be affected if the cotton balls came unexpectedly from different directions? Determine this by repeating the experiment, but have two people throw cotton balls at odd times from different directions at a person shielding his or her face with a plastic sheet. **Science Fair Hint:** Photographs of this experiment can be used as part of a project display, along with a summary of the results.

SHOW TIME!

1. The hair in a cat's ears can detect the slightest air movement. This allows the cat to respond to movements that are even too slight to produce sounds or to catch its eye. Test the sensitivity of human hair by asking a helper to look away as you gently move your hand back and forth against the ends of hairs on your helper's head and arm. Did your helper feel the movements?

2. Do organisms other than mammals have reflex actions? Earthworms do not have obvious sense organs, such as a nose or eyes, but they do have a nervous system that responds to stimuli such as touch or odors. Place several worms on a moist paper towel, and record their response to being touched with the end of a string. Photographs along with a summation of the responses can be displayed. (*Note: Approval for using living*

organisms in your science fair project may be needed. Check with your teacher before beginning this experiment. Upon completion of the experiment return the worms to their natural environment.)

3. What are some other common reflex actions in humans? You can display diagrams showing reflex actions that happen as a result of:
- being startled
- tapping the soft spot on your knee, below the kneecap
- touching something sharp, like a tack

CHECK IT OUT!

Reflex action causes animals to jerk away from heat before actually feeling the pain. Find out about the protective short-circuit path taken by nerve impulses that produces a reflex act. A diagram along with your explanation of the movement of the nerve impulses can be displayed.

3

OOPS!

How long does it take you to catch a falling object?

MATERIALS
table and chair
helper
ruler

PROCEDURE

1. Sit on the chair with your forearm on the tabletop and your writing hand extending over the edge of the tabletop.

2. Ask your helper to hold the ruler so that the bottom of the stick (the zero end) is just above your hand.

3. Place your thumb and index finger on either side of, but not touching, the bottom of the ruler.

12

4. Ask your helper to drop the ruler through your fingers without telling you when it is going to be dropped.

5. After the ruler is released, try to catch it as quickly as possible between your thumb and fingers.

6. Observe the number on the ruler just above your thumb. Record this number as the reaction distance.

RESULTS

The distance the ruler falls varies with each individual.

WHY?

The reason that the reaction time will vary with individuals is that when the ruler begins to fall, a message is sent to the brain. Like a computer, the brain takes this input information and, in fractions of a second, sends a message telling the muscles in the hand to contract. The distance the ruler falls can be different for each individual because it depends on the time it takes for these impulses to be sorted out by the brain and the output message to be received by the hand's muscles. The sensory nerves in the eye start this relay of messages called **nerve impulses.** The first stop is in the largest section of the brain called the **cerebrum.** The cerebrum is where all thoughts occur and where input from sensory nerves is interpreted. The cerebrum sends a message (nerve impulse) to another section of the brain called the **cerebellum.** The cerebellum brings together all the muscle actions that are necessary to grasp the ruler. This does not have anything to do with how smart you are; instead it compares differences in hand-eye coordination.

LET'S EXPLORE

1. Would practice change the reaction time? Repeat the experiment ten times. Record the reaction time for each trial in a chart similar to the one on page 14 and plot the data on a graph.

2. Would using a different hand affect the results? Change hands and repeat the experiment. Compare the differences in the improvement of the reaction times for the two hands.

Wade's Data Chart

Trial Number	Reaction Distance	Trial Number	Reaction Distance
1	18 inches (45 cm)	6	11 inches (28 cm)
2	14 inches (36 cm)	7	10 inches (25 cm)
3	12 inches (30 cm)	8	9 inches (23 cm)
4	12 inches (30 cm)	9	9 inches (23 cm)
5	11 inches (28 cm)	10	8 inches (20 cm)

3. Would distractions affect the results? Have a second helper to ask questions during the experiment. The questions could be simple math problems or anything that requires enough thinking to be distracting. Compare the reaction times with and without distractions.

4. Does the age of the experimenter affect

Wade's Reaction Time

the reaction time? Ask people of different ages to perform the experiment. **Science Fair Hint:** Photographs taken during the experiment along with graphs representing the results can be displayed.

SHOW TIME!

Can the reaction time of animals other than humans be influenced? Find out how dogs, horses, whales, and other animals are trained. A report about training animals can be part of a project. Include in the report answers to such questions as:

- What stimuli are used to encourage these animals to respond?
- Which animals respond the fastest?

All living organisms are constantly responding to stimuli around them. Stimuli are things that cause a response in a living organism. A cat hears a bird chirping, and its ears send a message to the brain. The cat may respond to the stimulus (the bird's chirp) in different ways—raising its ears, twitching its tail, or standing alert. Observe and discover other common responses made by animals around you. A diagram, like the one for the cat, can be used to represent the stimulus-response behavior of the animals.

CHECK IT OUT!

How do drugs and alcohol affect reaction time? Good sources for information about the affects of drugs would be your teacher, parent, school nurse, and/or physician.

"HEARING" WITHOUT EARS

PROBLEM

How do newts and salamanders hear without external ears?

MATERIALS
metal pie pan
table salt
metal spoon

PROCEDURE

1. Place the pie pan upside down on a table.

2. Sprinkle a very thin layer of salt over the upturned bottom of the pan.

3. Tap on the upturned bottom of the pan with the spoon.

4. Observe and record any difference in the movement of the salt crystals.

RESULTS
Tapping on the pan causes the salt crystals to move around.

WHY?
The molecules in the pan that is struck by the spoon start to **vibrate** (move back and forth). As these molecules move, they bump into neighboring molecules and start them moving, but with slightly less energy. This continues until there just is

not enough energy to cause the neighboring molecules to vibrate. Newts and salamanders that walk on land are able to "hear" by feeling vibrations from the surface they stand on. A slender muscle connects the shoulder blade (scapula) to bones set in a thin membrane of the ear cavity in the head. The

vibrations from the surface travel up the bone in the front leg to the shoulder blade, through the muscle, and on to the ear. Sounds close to the animal produce stronger vibrations, just like the greater movement of the salt crystals close to the tapping.

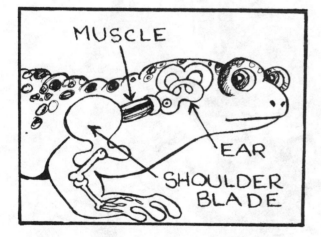

LET'S EXPLORE

1. Does the surface being tapped affect the vibrations? Repeat the experiment by placing the salt grains on different surfaces—a cardboard box, a wooden table, a plastic dish.

2. How does the distance from the tapped area affect the vibrations? Repeat the experiment tapping on the side of the pan farther from where the salt crystals are spread.

SHOW TIME!

1. How do other creatures without external ears, like fish, "hear"? Fish have a lateral line that runs down the side of their body. It is believed that this line of nerve receptors detects pressure and sound that travel through the water. Demonstrate the movement of waves through water by pouring 1 inch (2.5 cm) of water into a rectangular glass baking dish. Place the dish under a desk lamp and gently touch the surface of the water. Observe and record the movement of the water. Tap on the side of the dish, and determine if the sound is transmitted through the water.

Display photographs of the experiment as part of your project.

2. Birds have a keen sense of hearing. Owls can hear and locate their prey in the dark. The robin seems to be able to hear the movement of earthworms underground. Discover more about the ability of birds to receive sound. Display pictures of birds along with any unusual hearing abilities you have noted.

3. Elephants have very large ears and are able to hear faint sounds. Donkeys have the ability to move their ears and are alerted by the slightest noise. Discover more about the size and shape of external ears and how they affect the ability to hear. Display pictures of animals with various sizes and shapes of ears, and indicate their ability to hear.

5

FACE FORWARD

PROBLEM

What type of vision do animals have if their eyes face forward?

MATERIALS

2 sheets of notebook paper
cellophane tape

PROCEDURE

1. Roll each sheet of paper into a 1-inch (2.5 cm) tube. Fasten the edge of the paper with cellophane tape.

2. Hold the tubes to your eyes as you would a pair of binoculars.

3. Keep both of your eyes open.

4. While looking through both tubes, slowly move the far ends of the tubes together until you see one clear image of the object being viewed.

5. Close your left eye, and make note of what your right eye sees through the tube.

6. Close your right eye, and make note of what your left eye sees through the tube.

RESULTS

Each eye does not see exactly the same thing. The right eye views more of the right side of the object, and the left eye views more of the left side of the object.

LEFT
EYE VIEW

RIGHT
EYE VIEW

WHY?

The position of the eyes is very important. An animal that hunts for its food has its eyes facing forward on the front of its head like your own eyes. In this position, objects are viewed from two different angles. The two images are projected on the back portion of the eye (the retina) where they overlap. The overlapping images are interpreted by the brain as one clear, three-dimensional picture. The ability to combine images viewed by two eyes is called **binocular vision.**

SHOW TIME!

1. A chameleon's eyes face forward, but the eyes can move independently of each other when searching for food. What might the world look like through the roving eyes of a chameleon? Move the far ends of the tubes in different directions—up and down, left and right. Observe and record what you see. You should know that when this animal prepares to take aim with its tongue to capture its prey, the eyes face forward, giving the animal good distance judgment.

2. How does binocular vision produce a three-dimensional view? Discover how the overlapping of two images produces a three-dimensional picture by holding this book so that the tip of your nose touches the dot in the diagram. Keep both eyes open. Look straight forward as you slowly turn the book in a counterclockwise direction and watch the car travel up the path. Design other diagrams and use them

as part of a project display. Make sample copies for project observers to turn so that they can see the objects move.

3. How good is your peripheral vision (your sideview vision)? Your eyes, like those of other animals with eyes facing forward, have about a 180-degree angle of vision. Test your peripheral vision by standing in the center of a circle. Ask a helper to start from a point on the circle behind you and to slowly walk around the circle. Continue to look forward, not moving your eyes to the right or left. A mark is to be made on the circle when you first see your helper and again when he or she moves out of view on the opposite side. Test the angle of peripheral vision of other people. Photographs taken during this experiment can be used as part of your project display.

CHECK IT OUT!

Horses have eyes so placed that they can see all around their heads. The eyes of owls remain stationary, but their heads rotate 180 degrees, so they, too, can view the entire world around them. It is difficult to sneak up on an animal that sees from all angles. Discover more about the position of animal eyes and how this position affects an animal's life.

REFLECTORS

6

PROBLEM

Do cats' eyes glow in the dark?

MATERIAL

scissors
construction paper
empty coffee can (inside
    bottom must be shiny)
masking tape
flashlight

PROCEDURE

1. Cut a circle from the construction paper large enough to cover the end of the can.

2. In the center of the paper circle, cut a long oval opening.

3. Tape the paper circle over the open end of the can. This is a model of a cat's eye.

4. In a darkened room, hold the can at arm's length and at eye level in front of you with the paper end facing you.

5. Look toward the oval opening in the paper, and record your observations.

6. Hold the flashlight in front of your face with the light pointing at the oval opening in the paper circle.

7. Again look towards the oval opening, and record your observations.

RESULTS

The can is not very visible in the darkened room. When a flashlight is shined at the can, the shiny bottom of the can as well as the paper glows.

WHY?

Cats' eyes do not "glow" in the dark. The glow from the animal's eyes is due to the reflection of external light. The back of each cat's eye has mirrorlike cells that, like the bottom of the coffee can, reflect light. These cells are filled with a chemical called **guanine** that reflects even the smallest amounts of light and thus floods the eyeball with light, causing them to glow. The eyes do not appear to glow during the day because the oval-shaped slit in the animal's eyes (called the **pupil**) is only slightly open. Any light reflected during the day is not noticed because of the brightness of the sun's light. At night, the pupil opens exceptionally wide, allowing more light from a flashlight or other external light source to enter and be reflected from the back surface of the eye. The reflected light makes the eyes seem to glow in the dark.

LET'S EXPLORE

Does the size of the pupil (dark opening in the eye) affect the glow of the cat's eye? Change the size of the oval slit in the

paper circle and repeat the experiment. **Science Fair Hint:** Display the paper circles used in order of their ability to produce a glow.

SHOW TIME!

1. Why does the pupil of the cat's eye open more at night? In dim light or darkness, the muscles in the front of the eye of all animals relax, causing the opening in the eye to enlarge. To observe

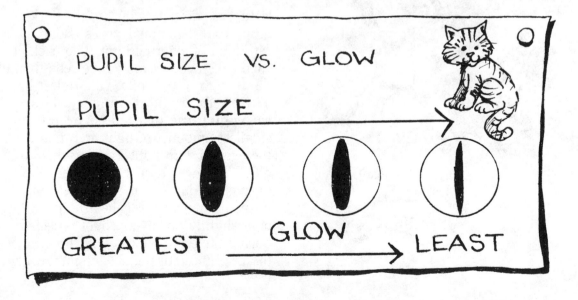

the effect that light has on the size of an eye's pupil, sit in a brightly lighted room for two minutes. Keep one eye tightly closed and the other eye open. Observe the pupil of the open eye by looking in a mirror. Open the closed eye and immediately observe the size of the pupil. Notice and record the difference in the pupil sizes of each eye. Use photographs of you as you perform this experiment. Drawings showing the size of your pupils can also be part of your project display.

2. Humans and other animals with good day vision have a thin layer of black tissue, called **choroid,** on the back surface of their eyes. Does the choroid layer reflect light? Cover the shiny bottom of the can with a piece of black construction paper and repeat the experiment. Use the materials and the results as part of a project display.

CHECK IT OUT!

Nocturnal hunters (animals that hunt at night) tend to have a long, oval-shaped pupil, while daytime prowlers have a round pupil. Find out how the shape of the pupil affects an animal's ability to see.

"SEEING" WITHOUT EYES

PROBLEM

Do earthworms "see" white light?

MATERIALS

scissors
ruler
shoe box with lid
paper towels
10 earthworms (can be
    purchased at a bait shop)
desk lamp

PROCEDURE

*Note: Obtain permission from your teacher
to use live animals as part of your project.*

1. Cut 4 inches (10 cm) from one end of the lid of the shoe box.

2. Moisten a paper towel with water and place it in the bottom of the box.

3. Position 10 earthworms at one end of the shoe box. Try to separate the worms as much as possible on the bottom of the box. Put the lid on the box so that the opening is over the worms.

4. Place a desk lamp so that its bulb is 18 inches (45 cm) above the open end of the box. Shine the light in the open end of the shoe box.

5. Observe the worms for 60 minutes.

EARTHWORMS   PAPER TOWEL

RESULTS

The worms start crawling around immediately. Some move toward the dark end of the box, and others begin to move under the paper towel. At the end of the 60 minutes, all or most of the worms have crawled away from the lighted area. All or most are in the shaded end of the box. A few may have huddled together under the paper towel near the lighted end of the box.

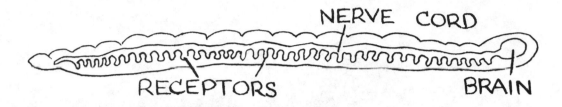

NERVE CORD

RECEPTORS

BRAIN

WHY?

The opening in the lid allowed white light from the lamp to enter the box. Earthworms do not have eyes to see light, but they move away from areas lighted by white light. An earthworm has a nervous system that responds to different stimuli, such as light. It has a brain at the front end of its body, and a large nerve cord extending the full length of the body. Each segment of the worm has nerve receptors leading out from the main nerve cord. White light stimulates these receptors, and a message is sent to the brain, resulting in the worm moving to a less lighted area.

LET'S EXPLORE

1. Is an earthworm's nervous system sensitive to different colors of light? Cover

the open end of the box with colored cellophane. In order to produce distinct colors of light in the box, cover the hole in the lid with four layers of each color of

FOUR LAYERS OF CELLOPHANE

cellophane tested. **Science Fair Hint:** Photographs can accompany the results of each test, and this information can be used as part of a project display. The testing box without the earthworms should also be displayed.

2. Is it possible that it's the heat from the lamp to which the earthworm is responding? Remove the heat factor by using a flashlight as the light source (a flashlight does not produce much heat). Prepare the lid by putting a circular hole in one end. The hole should be smaller than the end of the flashlight. Repeat the experiment using only the light from the flashlight for the white light source, and place the layers of colored cellophane under the light to test for responses to colored light.

SHOW TIME!

1. Is it possible for animals to "see" in complete darkness? Some snakes, including boas and vipers, are able to pick up infrared signals from warm objects by a pair of special heat-seeking eyes called **pit organs.** Discover how these pit organs respond to infrared heat. Display pictures of snakes with pit organs. Find and display a picture taken with special film sensitive to infrared heat.

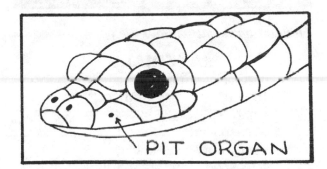

2. Bats are able to fly in complete darkness by emitting sound waves that bounce, or reflect, off objects. The reflected sound waves, or **echoes,** heard by the bat allow it to sense the position and size of objects and, thus, "see" in the dark. This is called **echolocation.** Explain and diagram how the process works, and find examples of other creatures that use echolocation.

8

TOOTHLESS

PROBLEM

How do birds eat without teeth?

MATERIALS
needlenosed pliers
10 sunflower seeds in shell
cup
1 teaspoon (5 ml) water
heavy-duty plastic bag
1 teaspoon (5 ml) aquarium
   gravel

PROCEDURE

1. Use the pliers to break open the shells of 10 sunflower seeds.

2. Separate the seeds from the shells.

3. Discard the shells, and place the seeds in the cup.

4. Add 1 teaspoon (5 ml) of water to the cup containing the seeds.

5. Allow the seeds to soak for 30 minutes.

6. Place the wet seeds in the plastic bag.

SEEDS

SHELLS →

sunflower SEEDS

7. Add the aquarium gravel to the plastic bag.

8. Place the bag between the palms of your hands.

9. Rub your hands back and forth to cause the gravel to grind against the seeds inside the bag.

10. Observe the seeds after grinding them with the stones for one minute.

RESULTS

The seeds are ground into a mush by the stones.

WHY?

Birds do not have teeth to grind their food, but they are able to daily digest large amounts of food to meet their high energy requirements. Birds that eat seeds have strong beaks to crush the shells and then remove the softer inner seeds. These seeds are swallowed and enter a **crop** (a sacklike structure in the throat of many birds) where they are stored and softened. Further softening takes place after the seeds are transferred to the stomach of the bird. The softened seeds then move on into a special organ called a gizzard that has a rough lining and strong muscles. Birds swallow small pebbles that stay in the gizzard. The muscles of the gizzard move the stones and the seeds around so that the food swallowed by the bird is ground up, or "chewed," by the stones, just as the seeds were ground by the aquarium gravel. The ground mushy seeds are at last moved to the intestine, where the nutrients are picked up by the blood and taken through the body. The constant grinding wears away small pieces of the stones, which mix with the ground mush and move into the intestines and are finally eliminated as waste from the bird's body. More stones are swallowed when older ones wear away.

LET'S EXPLORE

1. Would the size of the pebble swallowed

by the bird affect the way its gizzard will grind the food? Repeat the experiment using stones larger than aquarium gravel.

2. Can a seed in its shell pass through a bird's digestive system without being broken? Repeat the experiment without breaking the shells open.

SHOW TIME!

1. How do animals without gizzards or teeth grind their food? Some, like baleen whales, do not grind their food at all. The food is swallowed, and enters the stomach

where it is slowly digested. The baleen whale is the largest animal on earth and eats some of the smallest organisms. This creature lacks teeth but has rows of bones (called **baleens**) hanging from the roof of its mouth. These bones act like giant strainers. The whale moves through the water with its mouth open taking in huge quantities of water. Then it closes its mouth and pushes the water out through the baleens. Tiny shrimp and plankton are caught and swallowed. Demonstrate this capturing of tiny food particles by stirring loose tea leaves in a large bowl of water. Drag a tea strainer through the water and lift it out. Water drips out, leaving bits of tea leaves on the strainer. Pictures of baleen whales can be used as part of a project display along with photographs of this experiment. A summary of how the whale catches its prey should accompany the pictures.

2. Sparrows, finches, and grosbeaks are examples of birds that have exceptionally strong bills that are able to crack the hard shells of seeds. Find out more about the bills of different birds, and show examples of bills that are used for crushing, tearing, probing, and skimming. Display pictures of

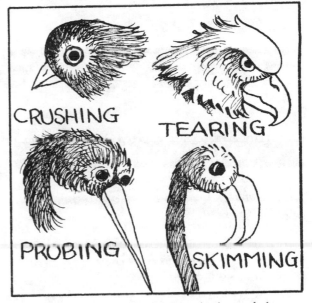

these bill types with a description of the food eaten by a bird that has each bill type.

CHECK IT OUT!

All animals with teeth do not grind their food. Snakes catch prey with sharp teeth and swallow it whole. Check out more about animals such as alligators that use their teeth not to chew with but to hold and kill their prey.

9

WARM-BLOODED

How is water used to lower an animal's body temperature?

MATERIALS

masking tape
marking pen
2 clear glasses
water
2 thermometers
1 bowl
freezer

PROCEDURE

1. Use the masking tape and marking pen to label the glasses #1 and #2.

2. Fill both glasses one-half full with warm water from a faucet.

3. Place a thermometer in each glass.

4. Allow the glasses to stand undisturbed for one minute.

5. Read and record the temperature shown on each thermometer.

6. Set glass #1 in the bowl.

7. Add cold water from the faucet so that

there are about 2 inches (5 cm) of water in the bowl.

8. As soon as the cold water is in the bowl containing glass #1, place glass #2 in the freezer and shut the door.

9. At the end of one minute, read and record the temperature shown on each thermometer.

RESULTS

The temperature of the water in glass #1 decreased more quickly than did the temperature of the water in glass #2.

WHY?

The body temperature of a cold-blooded animal changes with the temperature of its environment, but a warm-blooded animal maintains a constant body temperature regardless of the temperature outside its body. To regulate its temperature, a warm-blooded animal must increase heat loss from its body in hot weather and reduce heat loss during cold weather. One method of increasing heat loss is by bathing, wading, or standing in cold water. The water conducts heat from the animal's body more rapidly than does air. Your experiment demonstrated that heat energy in the water inside glass #1 moved out into the cooler water surrounding the glass. Heat energy in the water inside glass #2 also moved out into the air surrounding the glass but at a slower rate. This movement of heat energy from one substance to the next is called **conduction.** Water is a faster conductor of energy than air is.

LET'S EXPLORE

1. Would moving water affect the rate of cooling? Repeat the experiment using a wooden spoon to stir the water in the bowl. Would animals be cooled faster in a running stream or still pond?

2. Would placing icy water in the bowl have affected the rate of cooling? Repeat the experiment placing ice cubes in the bowl of water.

SHOW TIME!

1. Are there other methods of increasing heat loss from the body of animals? The hypothalamus (a part of the brain) activates nerve impulses that relax the walls of small arteries in the skin. This allows more blood to circulate to the surface of the body. Demonstrate that larger blood vessels allow more blood to pass through by using two coffee cans with plastic lids. In the lid of can #1, punch two small holes. In the lid of can #2, punch one small hole and a large hole. Half fill both cans with water and secure the lids. Measure the time it takes to fill a 5-ounce (150 ml) bathroom cup by pouring the water from can #1 through one of the small holes in the lid. Then measure the time it takes to fill another bathroom cup by pouring the water from can #2 through the large hole in the lid. The results along with diagrams and/or

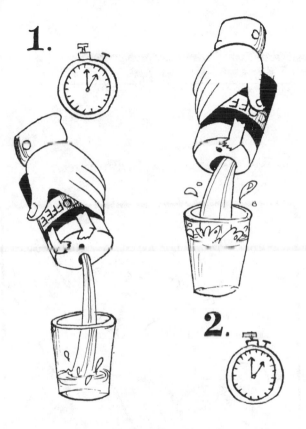

1.

2.

pictures taken during the experiment can be used as part of a project display.

2. How do animals conserve body heat when the environment is cooler than their body temperature? Cats, dogs, and bears are examples of animals that reduce exposed surface area such as their noses by curling into a ball. Warm air from their nose moves under and around the body. Humans often warm the exposed skin on their hands by blowing on them. Breathe onto the bulb of a thermometer to measure the warmth of your exhaled breath.

3. Birds tuck their legs under their feathers to cut down on heat loss during cold winter days. Sudden chills cause animals with hair to have "goosebumps" on their skin. These bumps raise the individual hairs, capturing air that better insulates the skin. Discover other methods of how warm-blooded animals regulate their body temperature to keep it constant. Use diagrams or photographs to display this information.

CHECK IT OUT!

The hypothalamus is the temperature regulator in warm-blooded animals. It has sensory cells that detect changes in blood temperature. Find out more about the functions of this special section of the brain.

10

COOLING OFF

PROBLEM

How do elephants use their ears to cool their bodies?

MATERIALS

3 × 5-inch (7.5 × 12.5-cm)
   index card
paper towel
water

PROCEDURE

1. Hold the index card about 4 inches (10 cm) above the skin on your arm.

2. Quickly fan the index card back and forth about 10 times.

3. Observe any cooling of your skin due to the fanning paper.

4. Wet the paper towel with water.

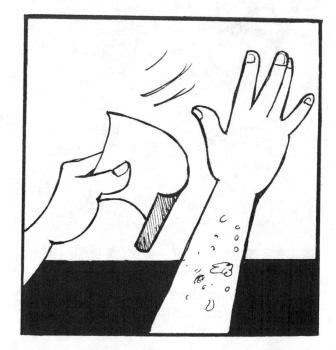

40

5. Rub the wet towel over the surface of your arm.

6. Hold the index card about 4 inches (10 cm) above your wet arm.

7. Quickly fan the index card back and forth about 10 times.

8. Again observe any cooling effect on the skin.

RESULTS

The wet skin feels cooler when fanned than does the dry skin.

WHY?

The cooling effect is due to the evaporation of the water from the skin. **Evaporation** occurs when a liquid absorbs enough heat energy to change from a liquid to a gas. The water takes energy away from the skin when it evaporates, causing the skin to cool. Elephants use their trunks to spray themselves with water; then they fan their bodies with their large ears. The fanning of their ears, like the index card, increases the flow of air across the skin. The moving air speeds the evaporation of the water and, thus, aids in the cooling of the skin.

LET'S EXPLORE

Would an elephant with bigger ears keep cooler? Determine the cooling effect of larger ears by repeating the experiment three times. Each time, increase the size of the index card or other piece of paper. **Science Fair Hint:** The different sizes of papers and their results can be used as part of a project display.

SHOW TIME!

1. Is it the moving air or the evaporation of the water that cools the skin? Demonstrate the cooling effect of evaporation by placing two thermometers on a table. Record the temperature shown on each thermometer. Wet a paper towel with water and place it over the bulb of one of the thermometers. Place a fan so that it blows across the bulbs of both thermometers. Record the temperature shown on each thermometer after five minutes. Photographs of this experiment with the results can be displayed.

2. Dogs do not have sweat glands in their skin to bring moisture to the surface to evaporate. They stick out their long, moist tongues and quickly draw air in through their noses and out their mouths. This is called **panting.** How does panting cool their bodies?

3. Polar bears and humans have about the same body temperature of 98.6 degrees Fahrenheit (37 degrees Celsius), but polar

bears often overheat because of their thick fur, skin, and fatty blubber. When a bear's body temperature begins to rise, the bear cools off by turning its face or its rear end into the wind. This cooling method is an example of conductive heat loss. In what other ways is heat lost from the bear's body by conduction?

HAIRY

11

PROBLEM

How does hair keep animals warm?

MATERIALS

box, at least 2 inches (5 cm)
    taller and wider than one
    of the jars
cotton balls
2 1-quart (1 liter) jars with
    lids
1-cup measuring cup
water
2 thermometers

PROCEDURE

1. Cover the bottom of the box with a layer of cotton balls.

2. Set one jar in the box.

3. Fill the box with cotton up to the top of the jar.

4. Use the measuring cup to add 2 cups (500 ml) of warm water from a faucet to each jar.

5. Stand a thermometer in each jar of warm water for one minute.

6. Read and record the temperature of the water in each jar.

7. Remove the thermometers, and seal each jar with a lid.

8. Quickly cover the jar in the box with a layer of cotton balls.

9. Close the lid on the box.

10. Leave the jars undisturbed for ten minutes.

11. Uncover the jars, and stand a thermometer in each jar.

12. Allow the thermometers to stand for one minute.

13. Read and record the temperature of the water in each jar.

RESULTS

The water in the jar that was placed in a box and surrounded by cotton stayed warmer than did the water in the uncovered jar.

WHY?

The cotton keeps the water in the jar warm because it prevents the heat inside the water from escaping too quickly. Much of the space around the jar in the box is filled with quiet, motionless air. The cotton balls are filled with air molecules. Heat from the warm water is conducted (transferred) to the cotton and the molecules of air trapped between the fibers of the cotton. Because the air is trapped, the heat is not carried away from the jar as it is in the uncovered jar. Molecules of air touching the uncovered jar pick up heat energy and take it away. Hair on animals, like the cotton fibers, traps air and prevents the heat produced by the body from escaping.

LET'S EXPLORE

1. Would a different covering around the jars affect the results? Repeat the experiment, but prepare two boxes and replace the cotton with feathers obtained from a pet store in one box and use woolen yarn instead of cotton in the second box. **Science Fair Hint:** The materials used, photographs, and diagrams along with the results from the experiments can be used as part of a project display.

2. Does the box affect the results? Change the experiment by using a woolen and a cotton sock to cover jars containing warm water. Measure the temperature of the

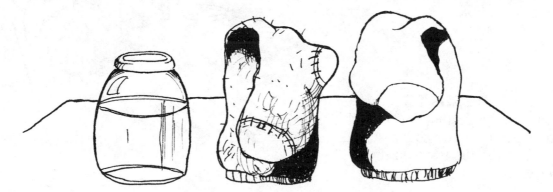

water before covering and at ten-minute time intervals for one hour.

3. Does an animal's hair keep it cooler in hot weather? Repeat the experiment using cold water. Determine if hair can act as an insulator to keep animals cool during hot summer weather.

SHOW TIME!

1. Nature provides many examples of energy conservation. During the winter, a bird stays warm by fluffing its feathers to trap air. To stay cooler during hot weather, the feathers are squeezed against the bird's body to remove the trapped air. What other ways do animals have to keep warm or stay cool?

2. "Goosebumps" cause individual hairs to stand on end. This keeps animals warmer because the standing hairs trap and hold a layer of still air around the body of the organism. What makes the hair stand erect, and what produces the bump the hair stands in? Use a diagram to show how "goosebumps" aid in warming the skin.

CHECK IT OUT!

The hairs on polar bears are a little like solar-heat collectors. They are hollow tubes that can trap light energy and funnel it to the skin of the bear. Find out more about the bear's hair.

12

FATTY INSULATORS

Does the fat layer under the skin keep an animal warm?

MATERIALS

2 7-ounce (210 ml) paper
  cups
shortening
2 thermometers
freezer
clock

PROCEDURE

1. Fill one paper cup with shortening.

2. Insert a thermometer into the cup of

shortening so that the bulb of the thermometer is in the center of the shortening.

3. Stand the second thermometer in an empty paper cup. *(Note: Lay the cup on its side if the weight of the thermometer tends to topple the cup over.)*

SHORTENING

4. Read and record the temperature shown on each thermometer. Then place the cups with their thermometers in the freezer and shut the door.

5. Read and record the temperature shown on each thermometer every three minutes until 30 minutes has passed.

6. Read the thermometers again after 24 hours.

RESULTS

In 30 minutes, the readings on the thermometer placed in the shortening changed very little, but the temperature inside the empty cup decreased rapidly. After 24 hours, both thermometers read the same.

WHY?

Heat energy moves from a warmer place to a colder place. When heat energy moves away from an object, that object becomes cooler. Its temperature gets lower. **Insulators** are materials that slow down the transfer of heat energy. The shortening, like the fat layer under the skin of animals, acts as an insulator and, thus, restricts the heat flow away from the warm inner body to the frigid air outside the body. The heat inside the shortening, like that in an animal's body, is lost, but, because of the insulating fat, the loss is very slow. Given enough time, the shortening finally freezes. Food eaten by animals provides energy that continuously replaces the lost heat. Thus, a constant body temperature is maintained.

LET'S EXPLORE

Are fatter animals warmer? Repeat the experiment using different thicknesses of shortening. The materials used and/or photographs of the experiment can be used along with the results as part of a project display.

SHOW TIME!

1. How do penguins keep their uninsulated feet and flippers from lowering their body temperature? A special system of blood vessels exists in the extremities of penguins. The arteries carrying warm blood to the feet and flippers are surrounded by veins carrying cold blood away from the feet and flippers. The cold

blood is warmed before it reaches the body, and the warm blood is cooled before reaching the feet. Demonstrate this energy exchange by placing a container of warm water inside a larger container of cold water. Keep a record of the temperature in both containers until no further changes are observed. Display the containers and an explanation of the results.

2. Does the color of an animal's feathers or hair affect its body temperature? Black objects absorb more light waves than do white objects. This absorption of the waves of energy causes the object's temperature to rise. Cover the bulb of one thermometer with white paper and the bulb of a second thermometer with black paper. Place the thermometers in direct sunlight and keep a record of their temperature readings for about 20 minutes. Photographs and diagrams along with the results can be used as part of a display.

BLACK PAPER

WHITE PAPER

CHECK IT OUT!

The male emperor penguin *incubates* (keeps warm and protected in order to hatch) the one egg laid by his female mate. He does this by rolling the egg onto his feet and covering it with a special fold of skin on the bottom of his stomach, which has several rolls of fat. Find out more about the nesting habits of different penguin species. How long does the male emperor stand with the egg on his feet? How do the nesting habits of Adélie and emperor penguins differ?

13

CURLY

What makes hair curly?

MATERIALS

scissors
ruler
sheet of typing paper
pencil

PROCEDURE

1. Cut a strip of paper 1 inch (2.5 cm) wide and 6 inches (15 cm) long.

2. Hold a pencil in the hand you write with.

3. Hold one end of the strip of paper between the finger and thumb of your free hand.

4. Place the pencil under the paper next to your finger, and slide the pencil down the paper with the strip tightly sandwiched between the pencil and the thumb of your writing hand.

5. Press the paper against the pencil with your thumb as you move the pencil down the paper strip.

6. Observe and record the shape of the paper strip.

RESULTS

The paper curls toward the side of the paper rubbed by the pencil.

WHY?

You probably think that paper is a flat surface. However, when you view it through a microscope, you can see the many fibers that make up the paper stick up and form hills and valleys across each sheet. Rubbing the paper causes these fibers to flatten out on the rubbed side. The paper, like a strand of hair, curls because one side is slightly flatter. The paper or hair strand will turn, or curl, toward the flatter side. Cross sections of hair strands reveal that straight hair is round and curly hair has an oval shape. The curlier the hair, the flatter is the cross-section view. One side of the hair strand must be slightly more flattened to cause the hair to curve around, thus forming spirals in the hair strand. The curls bend toward the flatter side of the hair strand as did the curls in the paper strip.

LET'S EXPLORE

Does the paper strip always curl toward the flatter side? Turn the curled paper over and rub the pencil down the opposite side several times. Explain why the first rubbing straightens the paper and continued rubbings cause the paper to curl

in the opposite direction. **Science Fair Hint:** Photographs showing the paper before and after the rubbings along with the paper strip and the explanation can be used as part of a project display.

SHOW TIME!

1. Can a strand of straight hair be curled by rubbing one side? With the permission of a friend with straight hair, borrow a long strand of hair. About 2 inches (5 cm)

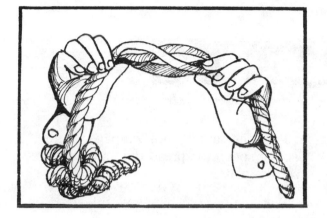

from the end, sandwich the hair strand between your index finger and thumbnail of your writing hand. Hold the short end with your free hand and move your nail down the hair. Observe the shape of the hair. Display the strand by taping one end to a sheet of paper. Use this and an explanation of why the hair changed its shape as part of a project display.

2. Would the texture of the hair affect it being curled? Use samples from different people and repeat the procedure of moving your thumbnail down the hair strand. Display all of the different samples along with explanations of why they each changed shape and a conclusion stating if texture affects the curling of hair.

3. Why does the kinky shape of wool make it good for making clothing? Hold one end of a 12-inch (30 cm) piece of wool knitting yarn in one hand. Pull on the opposite end with the other hand, and then let go. The piece stretches and springs together much like a rubber band. Untwist the strands of yarn and then let go. The strands spring back together. Make a diagram of the yarn to go with an explanation stating that woolen clothing feels comfortable because it stretches when you move and does not wrinkle greatly because the wool tends to spring back to its original shape.

CHECK IT OUT!

Hair from a horse's tail is very straight and is used to make paintbrushes. Discover more about the uses of straight and curly hair from animals. Display articles or pictures of items that use animal hair.

14

IMPRINTS

How were dinosaur tracks formed?

MATERIALS
½ cup (125 ml) flour
½ cup (125 ml) cornmeal
large mixing bowl
spoon
½ cup (125 ml) water
paper plate
8-inch (20 cm) square baking
  pan with water

PROCEDURE

1. Pour the flour and the cornmeal into a bowl and mix with the spoon.

2. Slowly add the water to the flour and cornmeal; stir until all the water is mixed in. This is your "homemade mud."

3. Pour the "mud" onto the paper plate. Use the spoon to spread the mud evenly over the plate.

4. Wet one of your hands with water from the pan.

5. Spread the fingers of the wet hand and press the palm side of that hand into the mud.

6. Remove your hand. You should see a good print of your hand. If you do not, do it again. Place the plate on a flat surface where it will not be disturbed.

7. Allow the mud to dry. It may take two to five days depending on the temperature and humidity of the air.

RESULTS
The mud dries, leaving a hard print of the shape of your hand.

WHY

The soft, homemade mud moved out of the way as you pressed your hand into it. The same thing happens to soft mud or sand when animals walk or crawl over it. If the imprint made in the soft mud is not disturbed before it dries, a hard print of the animal's track forms. Dinosaur tracks have been found in the Connecticut Valley and other places where these prehistoric animals walked in soft mud or sand. These rare tracks remained because they were covered with layers of dirt and sand and other sediment before the rest of the footprints were destroyed by winds, rains, or the pressure of other animals walking on the dirt. In time the deposit hardened into rock, and the track was trapped forever.

LET'S EXPLORE

1. Would the amount of water affect the print? Make different prints by using different amounts of water. Keep a record of the amount of water used with each mud mixture. Photographs of the imprints before and after drying can be used as part of a project display.

2. Would the type of dirt affect the print? Prepare different homemade mud samples by using different amounts of cornmeal and flour. First add more cornmeal and then repeat the experiment adding less cornmeal. Make the thickness of the mud in all samples as alike as possible. **Science Fair Hint:** Samples of the mud mixtures used can be displayed in small bottles along with photographs of the imprints and the summary stating which samples produced the best imprint.

SHOW TIME!

How can tracks be collected and studied? You can make plaster of paris (available at art supply stores) and pour it into animal tracks that you find in the dirt. *Note: Mix plaster in a throw-away container. Do not wash containers in the sink, because the plaster can stop up the drain.* Wait about 20 minutes for the plaster to dry. Then carefully lift the plaster from the dirt, and you should have a print. Present your ideas on what animals made the tracks and give your evidence why.

CHECK IT OUT!

Discover more about animal tracks and how to identify them. Find a book that shows what tracks are made by which animal.

15

GRIPPER

How do ridges on fingertips affect the ability to pick up objects?

MATERIALS
rubber gloves (the kind used
   for dishwashing)
assortment of small coins

PROCEDURE

1. Put one glove on the hand you write with.

2. Spread the coins out on a table.

3. Pick each coin up one at a time with the hand covered with the rubber glove. Place each coin back on the table before lifting the next coin.

4. Make note of the ease or difficulty in lifting each coin from the table's surface.

5. Note the texture of the fingers of the gloves.

6. Remove the glove from your hand.

7. Turn the glove that does not fit your writing hand inside out.

8. Put the inside-out glove on your writing hand.

9. Again pick each coin up one at a time with the hand covered with the rubber glove. Place each coin back on the table before lifting the next coin.

10. Make note of the ease or difficulty in lifting each coin from the table's surface.

11. Again note the texture of the fingers of the glove.

RESULTS

The coins are easily picked up when the glove is right side out, but are difficult or impossible to pick up when wearing the glove inside out.

WHY?

The fingertips are rough when the glove is on properly and smooth when the glove is inside out. The textured tips of the glove act like the ridged skin on the tips of your fingers, the ridges that cause fingerprints. The ridges in the rubber, as well as in your skin, increase friction and allow you to more easily pick up objects. **Friction** is the resistance to motion between two surfaces that are touching each other. Without the ridges on your fingertips, your fingers would tend to slide over objects, making it difficult to pick them up, just as it was difficult with the smooth tips of the inside-out glove.

LET'S EXPLORE

Does the pattern of the ridges on the fingertips affect their ability to grip surfaces? Repeat the experiment using rubber gloves with different patterns on the fingertips.

SHOW TIME!

1. Do the ridges on the bottom of your feet increase friction? Use shoes with

61

different sole surfaces such as tennis shoes and leather dress shoes to demonstrate the effect of ridges on friction. Push the shoes across a tiled floor and observe the resistance to motion (**friction**) of each shoe. Compare the friction of each shoe and label them from greatest friction to least friction. Repeat the experiment on floors with different surfaces. Take a photograph of the bottom of each shoe to display with your evaluation of the amount of friction each type of sole has.

2. How can a klipspringer (a mountain goat) jump and land on an area with about a 2-inch (5 cm) diameter? The hooves of this mountain climber are rubbery and rounded. You can demonstrate the ability of the klipspringer by slowly pitching two basketballs, one properly inflated and the other only partially inflated. Pitch the balls so that they land on a smooth surface. The fully inflated ball will move forward on the surface, but, because of more friction, the partially inflated ball stops when it hits.

3. Dogs slide around on slick floor surfaces. Why are cats not as likely to easily slide on the same surface? Discover how cats can pull their claws back into a sheath and, thus, expose only the soft pads of their feet. Diagrams of the feet of cats with their claws hidden and extended can be displayed.

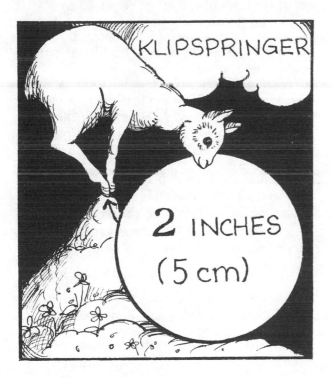

KLIPSPRINGER

2 INCHES (5 cm)

CHECK IT OUT!

The tarsier (a small mammal) leaps and easily clings to tree branches. The wiry fingers of these animals have pads on the ends that look like a rubber mat. Find out more about this creature and others that can grip well because of a high degree of frictional resistance of their fingers, hooves, or paws. Diagrams of the feet of different animals, indicating the ability of each to grip surfaces, can be displayed.

16

SUCTION FEET

How do starfish open the shells of mussels?

MATERIALS

4 suction cups with hooks
   (used to secure hanging
   crafts to windows)
water
refrigerator
helper

PROCEDURE

1. Dampen one of the suction cups with water. Press it on the surface of a refrigerator near the handle of the door.

2. Try to open the door by pulling outward on the suction cup.

3. Make note of the effort required to move the door.

4. Press a second suction cup (damp with water) next to the first cup.

5. Pull on both suction cups to try to open the refrigerator door. Make note of the effort required to move the door by pulling on two cups instead of one.

6. Dampen a third cup with water. Place it on the door near the others. Have a helper assist you in opening the door by pulling on one suction cup while you pull on the other two.

7. Attach the fourth cup, dampened with water. Again, with your helper's assistance, try to pull the door open.

8. Record the effort needed to open the door with each number of suctions cups.

RESULTS

It may be difficult or impossible to open the door with only one cup, but the effort needed to open the door decreases with the addition of another suction cup.

WHY?

Pressing a cup against the door forces the air out of the underside of the cup. The air in the room pushes and holds the flattened cup against the door's surface. Starfish

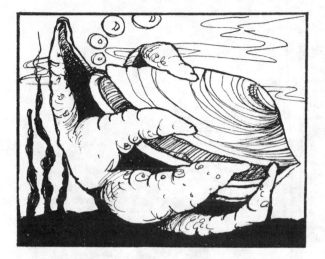

the effort of many feet pulling all at once, the halves of the shell are pulled apart.

Does the position of the starfish's feet make a difference in opening the shell? Demonstrate that less force is required if the feet are placed on the edge of the shell away from the hinge.

have rows of tube feet on the underside of their arms. Each foot is a small, hollow, fingerlike structure with a tiny sucker at the end. These suckers attach themselves to the shells of mussels in a way similar to the way the suction cups attach themselves to the refrigerator door. In the ocean, it is the pressure of the water, instead of air, that holds the suckers tightly against the shell. One sucker foot alone would not pull hard enough to open the tightly closed shell of a mussel. The starfish wraps its five arms around the shell, and groups of feet attach themselves to the shell. With

- Repeat the experiment placing the suction cups near the hinges of the refrigerator door.
- Make a model of a mussel shell by taping two plates together, and use the suction cups to lift the edges apart. Position the suction cups at various distances from the tape hinge.

SHOW TIME!

1. How do insects like ants walk on mirror-smooth surfaces or ceilings without suction pads on their feet? The legs of most insects end in a pair of claws with a pad between them. The pads are covered with numerous hollow hairs that are kept moist by a glandular secretion. The moist hairs on the feet of the insect wet the surface, and then the moist hairs stick to the wet surface. Demonstrate this type of holding power by wetting your finger with water and touching it to a small piece of paper. Lift the paper piece by raising your finger. Photographs of the lifting power of a wet finger can be displayed as part of a project display.

2. The toes of chameleons have adhesivelike tips that enable them to adhere to smooth surfaces. What other creatures have suction type-feet? Cut out pictures from magazines or draw each animal, and demonstrate why it needs the kind of feet it has.

CHECK IT OUT!

Snails and slugs leave a trail of slime. Find out where this slime comes from and how it helps the animal to cling to smooth surfaces.

CREATURE MOVEMENTS

17

PROBLEM

What causes the wavelike movement in an earthworm's body?

MATERIALS
Slinky™
smooth tabletop

PROCEDURE

1. Lay a Slinky on a table.

2. Hold the ends of the Slinky with your hands.

3. Hold your left hand still while your right hand pulls the other end of the Slinky out about 6 inches (15 cm).

4. Release the end of the Slinky held by your left hand.

5. Observe the movement of the Slinky.

RESULTS
The Slinky stretches and then springs back together. It moves forward about 6 inches (15 cm) from its old position.

WHY?
The Slinky, like an earthworm, moves by stretching out long and thin. Waves of motion are observed as the Slinky springs

forward. The earthworm also moves by a series of wavelike movements that pass from one end of the worm's body as it pulls up short. The wavelike motion that ripples through an earthworm's body is called **peristalsis.**

LET'S EXPLORE

Would the surface the Slinky is placed on affect its movement? Repeat the experiment, placing the Slinky on different surfaces such as a carpet, grass, or a sandy surface.

SHOW TIME!

Note: Obtain permission from your teacher to use live animals as part of your science project.

1. What keeps an earthworm from slipping backwards? Gently rub your finger over the bottom side of an earthworm. You should be able to feel the bristles. Place the earthworm on a moist paper towel, and gently pull the worm forward with your fingers. Be **very** gentle, or the end of the worm will break off. Photographs of this process can be used with the results as part of a project display. Return the earthworm to its natural environment after the experiment.

2. Demonstrate how the amount of air in a fish's swim bladder causes the fish to move up and down in water. Fill a plastic soft-drink bottle with water until it overflows. Partially fill a glass eyedropper with water and drop the eyedropper into the bottle of water. If the eyedropper sinks, remove it, squeeze some of the water out

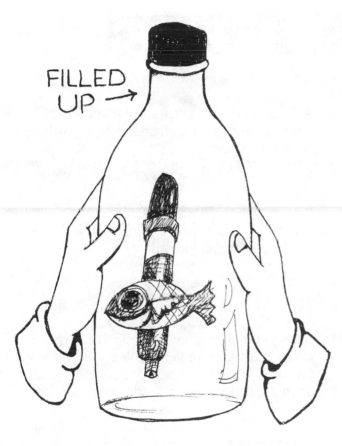

FILLED UP →

and put it back in the bottle of water. Put the cap on the bottle, and squeeze the sides of the bottle with your hands. Release the bottle. The moving of the water in and out of the dropper changes the volume of air inside the eyedropper and thus causes the dropper to rise and fall in the water. Attach a cardboard cutout of a fish to the eyedropper and display the bottle with your project.

3. Walrus, seals, and sea lions are **pinnipeds** (fin-footed). These creatures can use their fins to swim and to walk on land. Discover how other creatures move in water and in air and on land. Display pictures showing different ways that creatures move about.

CHECK IT OUT!

Some snakes move from side to side, while others move in a manner referred to as a caterpillar crawl. Find out how snakes make their way over the ground and through water.

POLKA DOTS

How do chameleons change colors?

MATERIALS
magazine with colored
   pictures
desk lamp
magnifying lens

PROCEDURE

1. Place the magazine under the light of a desk lamp.

2. Hold your face about 6 inches (15 cm) above one of the colored pictures in the magazine.

3. Close one eye. Use your open eye to look through the magnifying lens at the colored picture.

4. Move the lens back and forth between your eye and the magazine picture until a clear image forms.

5. Carefully study areas of different colors.

RESULTS
You will see that every color is a combination of colored dots.

WHY?
The color of a chameleon's skin, like the colors in the picture, is actually a combination of colors. The skin of this lizard has layers of cells called **chromatophores**. Each cell contains color matter called **pigment** and comes in different colors, including red, brown, yellow, and white. Special chromatophores called **melanophores** contain a dark pigment. These special cells have a center section with branches sticking out in all

directions. Temperature, light, and chemicals in the animal's body cause the pigment to expand and, thus, move out into the branches of the cell or to contract and concentrate in the center of the cell.

When the branches of the melanophores are empty, the color pigments in the other cells show through. When the branches are filled with the dark pigment, they hide some of the colors in the other cells. The combinations of the pigments result in skin colors including red, yellow, green, brown, and gray.

A CHAMELEON'S SKIN CELL

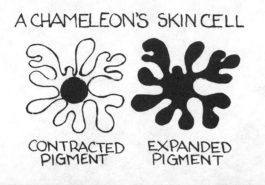

CONTRACTED PIGMENT   EXPANDED PIGMENT

LET'S EXPLORE

What color combinations make up the individual colors of red, yellow, green, brown, and gray? Repeat the experiment, recording the color combinations observed for the specific colors. **Science Fair Hint:** Use colored construction paper to prepare enlarged models of the color combinations viewed through the magnifying lens. Display the models.

SHOW TIME!

1. How do the different-colored dots look like one color? The brain receives the light from the separate color dots and blends them together. Demonstrate the blending of light from separate objects by using different colors of cellophane. Lay the colored pieces so that their edges overlap. Use the cellophane as part of a project display.

2. How does light affect the color of the chameleon's skin? In intense sunlight, the

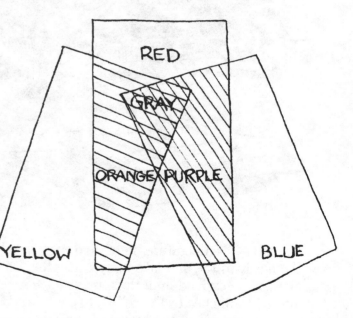

skin becomes darker, as does the skin of humans. In the absence of light, the skin becomes lighter. Since different colors of skin contain different amounts of pigment, ask several people with varying skin colors to wear a plastic bandage on one finger. Remove the bandage after several days and observe the color of the skin outside and inside the area covered by the bandage. Color photographs can be displayed.

3. Are the colors in a bird's feathers due to color pigment? Actually, the bright blue color of some bird's feathers results from the scattering of light waves. Tiny air bubbles in the feathers scatter the blue light coming from the sun, which results in the feathers appearing to be blue. You can demonstrate the scattering of blue light by filling a glass with water and adding one drop of milk to the water. In a darkened room, use a flashlight to direct a light beam through the center of the water. The water appears to be a grayish blue. If more blue waves were reflected, a brighter blue would be seen.

CHECK IT OUT!

An animal can be colored or can have patterns of colors that allow it to blend well with its background. This makes it difficult to see. Find out more about the protective coloration of creatures.

19

LUB-DUB

Why does the heartbeat of mammals make a sound?

MATERIALS

scissors
glue
construction paper
large thread spool
pencil
cellophane tape

PROCEDURE

1. Cut and glue a circle of construction paper over each end of the thread spool. Allow the glue to dry for several hours.

2. Use a pencil to punch a hole in the paper circles to line up with the hole in the spool.

3. Cut a smaller paper circle about 1 inch (2.5 cm) in diameter.

4. Center this small paper circle over the other paper circle on one end of the spool, and secure it on one side with a piece of tape about ¼ inch (6 mm) wide. This makes a flap over the hole.

5. With your mouth, blow through the hole in the spool end without the flap. This pushes up the paper flap on the other end.

6. Suck air back through the hole with enough force to cause the paper flap to hit against the top of the spool.

7. Repeat the blowing and sucking of air through the hole in the spool.

8. Listen to the sound made as the paper flap moves up and down.

BLOW OUT →

SUCK IN →

RESULTS

A swishing sound is heard when the air pushes the flap up, and a thumping sound results each time the flap hits the surface of the spool.

WHY?

In all mammals, the heart is a double pump. Each side of the heart has an upper and lower chamber. The top parts are called **atriums** and the lower parts are called **ventricles.** A one-way flap called a valve connects the upper and lower chambers. When the heart muscle relaxes, blood flows through the open valves from the atriums into the ventricles. When the heart contracts, the flap is closed with a thump. The valve prevents the blood from moving back into the atrium, and it is forced out of the heart through another opening. The opening and closing of the paper flap on the thread spool produces a sound like that made by heart valves. The sound from the valves can be heard through the tissues of the body and is often described as a lub-dub sound.

LET'S EXPLORE

Would a hole in the flap affect the sound? Repeat the experiment first with a small hole in the paper flap. Repeat several times with increasingly larger holes in the flap.

SHOW TIME!

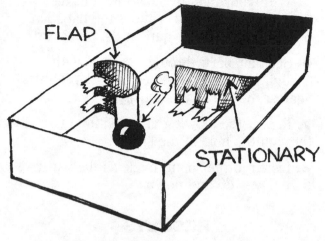

FLAP

STATIONARY

1. How can blood flow in only one direction in blood vessels? Veins and arteries both have valves. Build a model using a box and two flaps of stiff paper to demonstrate the movement of blood through the one-way valves in blood vessels. A marble can be used to represent blood. Tilt the container forward so that the marble hits the flap and opens it. Tilt the container backward, and the marble hits against the flap, closing it. Your model, along with diagrams of vessels, can be used as part of a project display.

2. How much blood moves with each heartbeat? This can vary with the size of the heart. In humans, the average is about

¼ cup (60 ml) per beat, or about 5 quarts (5 liters) per minute. Demonstrate the work done by the heart by using a ¼-cup (60 ml) measuring cup to transfer 5 quarts (5 liters) of water from one container to another. Remember that the job must be done in one minute. Dip the measuring cup into the water, and pour the water into the other container. Photographs of this experiment are the best way to display the procedure. Count each transfer to determine the number of times the heart would have to beat in one minute in order to pump 5 quarts (5 liters) of blood.

CHECK IT OUT!

1. Animals have hearts with two or more chambers that pump blood through their circulatory system. Discover more about the hearts of different animals. How do the hearts of fish, amphibians, mammals, and birds differ? What is the specific difference between the hearts of birds and mammals? Use diagrams of animal hearts as part of your project display.

2. Insect blood is usually greenish in color. Some insects have pulsating sacs in their knee joints that push the blood throughout the body. Find out more about the circulatory system of insects.

SUPER SPOUT

20

PROBLEM

What is in a whales's spout?

MATERIALS
hand mirror
freezer
paper towel

PROCEDURE

1. Place the hand mirror in the freezer for five minutes.

2. Open the freezer, and observe any fog forming in front of the freezer.

3. Remove the mirror from the freezer.

4. Wipe the mirror with the dry paper towel.

5. Hold the mirror about 2 inches (5 cm) from your mouth.

6. Breathe onto the mirror.

7. Observe the surface of the mirror.

RESULTS
The mirror becomes fogged with tiny droplets of water.

WHY?
Air in lungs is warm and moist. When it hits the cooler mirror surface, the moisture

open freezer or your smoky-looking breath outside on a cold day are both a result of condensation. The cooling of warm, moist air changes the water from a gas to a liquid. When small amounts of warm moist air are cooled, small droplets of water are formed. A whale's body cavity acts as a giant air storage tank. The condensing of such large amounts of warm, moist air upon exhaling results in a spout that looks like a geyser. The spray from the whale is a mixture of water and air.

in your exhaled breath condenses (changes from a gas to a liquid). The wisps of fog forming in the warm air in front of the

LET'S EXPLORE

1. Would making the mirror colder affect the results? Repeat the experiment, but leave the mirror in the freezer for a longer period of time.

2. What effect would warming the mirror have on the results? Repeat the experiment warming the mirror in sunlight.

SHOW TIME!

1. What causes the whale's spout to shoot so far into the air? Whales dive far below the water's surface. The weight of the water on the whale causes the air inside its body to compress, or get pushed into a small space. When the whale quickly surfaces and exhales, the gases expand and are pushed out with a great force. A spout of air and water shoots upward from the hole in the whale's head to about 50 feet (15 m). This can be demonstrated by spraying some of the contents of a spray bottle filled with water into the air. Squeezing the handle pushes the water out with a great force in the same way that the air shoots from inside the whale's body. Diagrams showing the spray bottle and a whale's spout can be used as part of a science project display.

2. A whale can exhale as much as 2000 quarts (2000 liters) of air. How many quarts (liters) can a human exhale? A gallon plastic milk jug holds 4 quarts (4 liters). Use this jug to measure the amount of air that you can exhale. Fill the jug with water and turn it upside down into a pan of water. With the assistance of a helper, place a clean aquarium tube inside the mouth of the jug. Take a normal breath, and then exhale through the tube. Pour the water left in the jug into a measuring cup to determine the amount of air that you exhaled. You could use a picturegram showing the number of quarts exhaled by different animals as a display.

3. The lungs of frogs are not very efficient. The frog's mouth acts as a bellows to pump air in and out of its lungs. Demonstrate this by exhaling and inhaling into a balloon. Diagrams of the change in the balloon's size as you exhale and inhale can be displayed and compared to changes in a frog's lungs.

CHECK IT OUT!

Respiration involves the exchanges of gases. Oxygen is the gas that enters the body cells, and carbon dioxide is the gas that leaves the cells. In animals with lungs, this gas exchange takes place in the lungs. Find out how the gas exchange take place in creatures without lungs, such as earthworms.

Arteries   Blood vessels that carry oxygen-rich blood away from the heart.

Atrium   Upper chamber of a heart.

Baleens   Rows of bones in the mouth of a baleen whale. The bones act like giant sieves to separate tiny shrimp and plankton from water.

Binocular Vision   The ability to combine images viewed by two eyes.

Capillaries   Tiny vessels connecting arteries and veins.

Cerebellum   The part of the brain that coordinates all the muscle actions.

Cerebrum   The part of the brain where all thought occurs and where input from sensory nerves is interpreted.

Choroid   A thin layer of black tissue in the eye that absorbs light rays.

Chromatophores   Cells that contain color pigment.

Cold-blooded   The property by which an organism changes its body temperature to match that of its environment.

Condensation   The changing of a gas into a liquid.

Conduction   Movement of energy from one substance to the next.

Conductor   A material through which energy moves freely.

Crop   A sacklike structure in the throat of many birds where food is stored and prepared for digestion.

Echolocation   System of seeing with sound by sending out sound waves and timing the returning echo.

Evaporation   The process by which a liquid absorbs energy and changes to a gas.

Friction   The resistance to motion between two surfaces that touch.

Gizzard   Organ found in animals such as birds and earthworms. It has a rough lining and strong muscles used to grind food with swallowed stones that remain in the gizzard.

Goosebumps   Constricted muscles that not only raise individual hairs but also form small bumps on the skin's surface.

Guanine   Chemical found in the back of the eye of night hunters, such as cats. Guanine reflects light, thus causing the eyes to appear to glow.

Heart   Muscular organ that pumps blood through the body of animals.

Hypothalamus   The brain center that controls body temperature and body functions such as appetite and sleepiness.

Infrared   Invisible rays of light beyond the red end of the visible spectrum that are emitted by hot bodies.

Insulator   Materials that slow down the transfer of energy.

Involuntary Movement   Movement of body parts without thinking.

Lungs   Saclike organ where oxygen enters the blood and carbon dioxide leaves the blood.

Melanophores   Special cells containing a dark colored pigment called melanin.

Molecules   Minute particles. The smallest portion of a compound.

Monocular Vision   Images seen by eyes that work independently.

Nerve Impulses   An electric-like message that travels from one nerve cell to another.

Pigment   Colored matter.

Pinnipeds   Fin-footed animals such as walrus, seal, and sea lions; able to use their fins to swim and to walk on land.

Pit Organ   Heat-sensing area on the skin that responds to infrared heat.

Pupil   Dark opening in the eye.

Reaction Time   Time required for an input message from sensory nerves to be sorted out by the brain and an output message to be received by responding muscles.

Reflex Action   An automatic movement that does not require thinking.

Retina   The light-sensitive layer in the back of the eye.

Solar Heat   Heat from the sun.

Spontaneous Generation   The theory that living organisms come from nonliving material.

Stimuli   Anything that causes a response in a living organism.

Sweat Glands   Organs that produce surface moisture, which evaporates, cooling the skin.

Valve   An opening leading from one area to another.

Veins   Blood vessels carrying oxygen poor blood toward the heart.

Ventricle   Lower chamber of the heart.

Vibrate   To move back and forth rapidly.

Voluntary Movement   Movement of body parts that requires thinking.

Warm-blooded   The property by which an organism maintains the same body temperature regardless of the temperature outside the body.

INDEX

HAVE MORE FUN WITH SCIENCE....

JOIN THE SCIENCE FOR EVERY KID CLUB!

Just fill in the coupon below and mail to:
FAN CLUB HEADQUARTERS/F. Nachbaur
John Wiley & Sons, 605 Third Avenue, New York, NY 10158

Name_____

Address_____

City_____ State_____ ZIP_____

Membership in the Science for Every Kid Club entitles you to a quarterly newsletter featuring science tidbits, games, and other experiments, plus other surprises...and it's free!!!   007

✂ -

More Exciting and Fun Science Activity Books from Janice VanCleave...

To order by Phone:

Mail To: John Wiley & Sons, Inc. 605 Third Avenue, New York, NY 10158 Attn: F. Nachbaur

___ ANIMALS (55052-3), @ $9.95
___ GRAVITY (55050-7), @ $9.95
___ MOLECULES (55054-X), @ $9.95
___ ASTRONOMY FOR EVERY KID (53573-7), @ $10.95
___ BIOLOGY FOR EVERY KID (50381-9), @ $10.95
___ CHEMISTRY FOR EVERY KID (62085-8), @ $10.95
___ EARTH SCIENCE FOR EVERY KID (53010-7), @ $10.95
___ MATH FOR EVERY KID (54265-2), @ $10.95
___ PHYSICS FOR EVERY KID (52505 7), @ $10.95
___ 200 GOOEY, SLIPPERY, SLIMY, WEIRD, AND
FUN EXPERIMENTS (57921-1), @ $12.95

**Call Toll-Free
1-800-CALL WILEY**

❏ Payment enclosed (Wiley pays postage & handling)   NAME_____

❏ Charge my __ Visa __ Mastercard __ Amex   ADDRESS_____

Card #_____ Exp. Date ___/___   CITY/STATE/ZIP_____

WILEY
Publishers Since 1807